Witness in Montgomery

WITNESS IN MONTGOMERY

A CONTEMPORANEOUS ACCOUNT OF THE 1983 'TODD ROAD INCIDENT'

HORACE RANDALL WILLIAMS

BLACK BELT PRESS

Montgomery

Black Belt Press
105 S. Court Street
Montgomery, AL 36104

Cataloging-in-Publication Data
978-1-961938-11-3 (paperback)
978-1-961938-12-0 (ebook)

This essay is excerpted from *Looking for the Heart of Dixie: Fifty
Years of Dispatches from the Deep South* (forthcoming from Black
Belt Press). The essay first appeared in the July 1983 (Vol. 5,
No. 4) issue of *Southern Changes* magazine, a publication of the
Southern Regional Council of Atlanta, Georgia. The SRC is
now defunct; its archives are at the Atlanta Public Library and
some digital holdings are at Emory University.

Printed in the United States of America

*The Black Belt, defined by its dark, rich soil, stretches across
central Alabama. It was the heart of the cotton belt. It was
and is a place of great beauty, of extreme wealth and grinding
poverty, of pain and joy. Here we take our stand, listening to
the past, looking to the future.*

July 1983

Not since the celebrated bus boycott of 1955–56 or the Selma March days of 1965 has the atmosphere in Montgomery, Alabama, been so charged with racial tensions. The immediate cause is a string of incidents involving blacks and the Montgomery police, but behind these cases looms a larger issue, Mayor Emory Folmar, a conservative Republican who was beaten decisively by George Wallace in the 1982 governor's election.

Folmar is both mayor and de facto police chief of Alabama's capital city, and his hard-line, love-it-or-leave-it attitudes on public safety, community development, redistricting and other issues have led to steadily deteriorating relations with the forty percent of Montgomery's population that is black, as well as with a growing number of whites. His critics, while recognizing that the recent police confrontations were serious incidents, charge that a more flexible personality and more responsive leader than Folmar would have prevented their escalation into a full-scale community crisis.

Now, the situation is reminiscent of the earlier civil rights era in this city known as the Cradle of the Confederacy. The

This article was published in 1983 in Vol. 5, No. 4 of Southern Changes, *the journal of the Atlanta-based Southern Regional Council.*

black churches are again the scene of mass meetings. The black leadership has held well-publicized but private strategy sessions from which has emerged an unusual—for recent years, at least—unanimity, including an economic boycott of the city's largest bank. Picket lines have been thrown up against a white-owned black radio station. Protest marches have been held. A cross has been burned in the yard of the spokesman for the black leaders.

Several incidents since the first of the year have contributed to the current situation. Most recently, an unarmed black man was killed in June by a white policeman responding to a report of a shooting in the neighborhood. In May, a black man who was apparently drunk but unarmed was killed by a black policewoman. In April, a white policeman seriously wounded an unarmed black man who was mistakenly thought to be an escaped prisoner.

The first and most controversial incident occurred in February when a group of black mourners was assembled in the deceased's home following the funeral. Before the night was over, two white plain-clothes policemen had been injured, one critically, and eight mourners arrested. The police say they identified themselves, were taken hostage and then beaten and shot. The mourners say the two whites did not identify themselves as police but kicked down the door to the house and charged in with their guns drawn, at which time the blacks disarmed them and then called the police. Later, the mourners say, more police arrived and the two whites tried to escape and shots were fired.

THE TWO ACCOUNTS VARY so widely that Montgomery citizens can only wait and hope that the upcoming trials will reveal the truth. However, the police department's early handling of the incident was seen by blacks and many whites as a gross over-reaction and an attempt to cover up possible improper conduct by the two officers. For example, Police Chief Charles Swindall held a pre-dawn press conference to denounce the mourners as "wild animals who had prey on their ground." He used the word *torture* to describe the treatment of the officers, said one of them had had his throat slashed requiring seventy-five stitches, and made other highly inflammatory comments.

This infuriated blacks, especially when the press later reported that the most serious prior offenses of any of the accused were traffic violations, that the officer's throat required ten stitches instead of seventy-five, and that one of the officers'

Mayor Folmar, second from left, and Chief Swindall, third from left, in a 1982 Montgomery Advertiser *photo.*

guns was missing, despite the fact that police had immediately surrounded the house and searched everyone present. Also, the police tape recorder was reported not to have worked when it should have automatically recorded radio transmissions and phone calls about the incident. In addition, there were allegations that the accused were beaten during interrogation.

On the other hand, many whites and some blacks criticized over-reaction by black leaders, too, notably the call by State Rep. Alvin Holmes for federal authorities to place the city under martial law. The circumstances of the incident cast grave doubt on the conduct of the police, mused many Montgomerians, yet there was no getting around the fact that two officers were seriously wounded. Why, asked whites, were there not some prayers for the two officers among the vigils and protests that were being held in the black community?

The matter of the missing tape recording from police headquarters was seen as similar to a mid-1970s scandal in which police wrongfully shot a black man, Bernard Whitehurst, then allegedly planted a gun on his body. The automatic tape recordings in that incident had been erased by the time the prosecutor asked for them, and ultimately the public safety commissioner, the mayor, and nearly a dozen police officers resigned or were fired.

The mayor at that time was James Robinson, and his resignation led to a 1977 *Former Mayor Jim Robinson.*

Montgomery's city council, 1975.

special election which was won by Emory Folmar, who had been the city council president. Ironically, Robinson is widely perceived by blacks as a basically decent man who was trapped in the Whitehurst scandal by accident, while Folmar is believed by many blacks to be *the* problem with the police department. In addition, Folmar is seen as being generally hostile toward black interests if not actively racist.

Robinson usually enjoyed good relations with the black community. In fact, Robinson was instrumental in changing the city's form of government in the early 1970s from a three-man commission, elected at-large, to the nine-district council, thus paving the way for the first black elected municipal officials in Montgomery history.

When the first council elections were held in 1975, four blacks and five whites were chosen, and the nine then selected Folmar as the council president. It was Folmar's first venture into elective politics, and from the council's first organizational meeting, he made it clear that he meant to be a force to be reckoned with.

His District Eight constituents were overwhelmingly white and among the city's wealthiest and most conservative residents. Through a combination of representing his district and exercising his own philosophy of government, Folmar was frequently at opposites with black council members on issues ranging from council appointments to the allocation of community development funds, In fairness to Folmar, it should be said that he was not alone—many council votes were split five to four along racial lines; but blacks resented Folmar most because he was not only council president but also its most powerful personality, and at least two of the white council members invariably cast sidelong glances at Folmar before raising their own hands during votes on controversial issues.

Two council debates are good illustrations. The first concerned community development money, which was intended by Congress to help eliminate what planners call urban blight. To the blacks on the city council, this meant the money should build sewers, sidewalks, street lights, and community centers in low-income areas, particularly in black low-income neighborhoods which had been neglected in all the decades past; Montgomery had several black neighborhoods as late as 1975 which still relied on outdoor privvies because sewer lines had never reached them.

Long battles were fought over this money and in the end many sewers and sidewalks were built. But the community development funds also helped build a golf course at a recreation complex located on the eastern edge of Montgomery near the suburbs where white residents have been steadily relocating since World War II. Community development money was also used for three neighborhood parks built in predominantly white residential areas which definitely were not blighted. Folmar did not win these projects without help, but he was instrumental in their passage and his attitude was interpreted by blacks as one of "I don't care what Congress said, we whites, poor or not, are also getting some of that government money."

A second case which increased the black council members' distaste for Folmar arose when blacks moved to rename a street in honor of Martin Luther King Jr. The avenue in question, Jackson Street, was the site of King's home for the years that he was the pastor of the Dexter Avenue Baptist Church; this was the house that was bombed in 1956 while Coretta King and child were inside (they were uninjured). Folmar spoke and voted against the renaming and then introduced a compromise which would have named after King a section of Interstate 85, which passes through the city. This debate had occurred before, in the early seventies when Montgomery still had a three-man commission form of government, and the Interstate compromise initially failed because of opposition from state officials. The issue then took on a new significance after blacks had achieved voting power in city government.

One argument was that it would be wrong to dishonor Andrew Jackson in order to honor King, so the Interstate memorial was an alternative that coincidentally would be even more visible. Getting the memorial was symbolically very important to Montgomery blacks and the street renaming was the first major question with racial implications to come up after the four black council members had taken their seats. The new black members were surprised and disappointed that the white council members had felt it was necessary to put up a fight on the issue, and the black members were not satisfied totally with the Interstate memorial since it was not city property. But they accepted the compromise anyway, only to discover that federal highway regulations prohibit the naming of interstates for individuals. Rightly or wrongly, many observers, white and black, believed that Folmar had known this fact all along and had deliberately led the council down a rabbit trail. Ultimately, blacks in the Alabama legislature pushed through a resolution and overcame the federal obstacles, and today all who pass through Montgomery on I-85 see a huge green sign proclaiming a three-mile stretch of the interstate as Martin Luther King Jr. Expressway. But the incident seemed to decrease Folmar's stature in the black community, and relations with his black colleagues on the city council have continued to worsen since he became mayor and his power increased.

GUNG-HO, STUBBORN, FIERCELY COMPETITIVE, hardworking, and capable are terms which are regularly used to describe the mayor. Hard-headed, macho, dictatorial, intolerant, devious, racist, overly aggressive, and paranoid are some others.

Employees at city hall say that if Folmar were judged on administrative ability and dedication alone, he would rank among the best mayors any city could want. He is at his desk most days before other employees have taken their morning showers. He is personally wealthy—before entering politics he was a shopping center developer—and draws only a token dollar a year as his mayoral salary (though a recent letter-to-the-editor writer argued that he is overpaid).

He is an ex-Army officer who was a highly decorated hero of Korea. He still keeps himself in rock-hard physical condition and takes a military approach to organization and discipline. Nowhere is this more apparent than with the police, and it is in the area of law enforcement that his critics are most severe. The critics come from both inside and outside the police department.

Outside critics charge that Folmar believes, and expects everyone else to believe, that the police are always right; that he has encouraged an us-versus-them mentality; that he tries to run the department himself, and that the net result has been an increase of incidents of harassment by police, especially of blacks and gays.

"Just call our city Fort Montgomery and the mayor our commander-in-chief," comments Joe Reed, a black city councilman who has been Folmar's most persistent opponent in city government and who is also the head of the Alabama Democratic Conference, the state's leading black political organization.

Adds Willie Peak, the white president of the city council, "Most whites recognize there could be possible wrongs on both sides (of the February confrontation). Most whites are concerned about the 'we can do no wrong' attitude of the police."

Critics inside the police department also fault Folmar for trying to run it like a military battalion with himself as general; for imposing his decisions over those of experienced, career police professionals, and for making promotions contingent on an officer's personal loyalty and chumminess with the mayor.

Since Folmar came to power, several high-ranking police officials have retired from the department rather than accept the mayor's tight control. Their privately stated grievances range from favoritism in promotion, to what they view as a ridiculous obsession with spit and polish, to Folmar's actual interference with field operations. It is true that Folmar has personally shown up at all hours of day or night to participate in or take charge of on-the-scene police work, and that the officers who are detailed as his bodyguards move rapidly through the ranks, often bypassing officers of greater experience. To give the example of just one officer, an example related by other police, Folmar acknowledged the good work of the officer yet refused to promote the man because "you're not loyal to me."

Folmar *is* the police chief, observed one ex-officer. "He

personally promotes; Chief (Charles) Swindall doesn't have the gumption or the power to do anything about it. Chief Swindall should have retired when Folmar was reelected." Both current and ex-officers view this as a bitter irony because they consider Swindall to be an excellent police officer and actually a better chief than the man he replaced.

Folmar's personal pistol-packing gave rise to the Montgomery joke: "Question: Why is the Mayor's pistol chrome-plated? Answer: So it won't rust in the shower."

The police themselves tell and laugh at this joke, but they are less amused by Folmar's parade inspections and pep talks. "These are grown men he's having out there standing at attention. This isn't boot camp," observed an ex-officer.

Ex-police are also critical of the department's low salaries and note that Montgomery taxpayers routinely spend five thousand or more dollars to send a new officer through Police Academy training only to have him leave for a better paying job after a year or two on the force. Many ten-, fifteen-, and even twenty-year veterans are also tempted out of police work for higher salaries with detective or security agencies or state government jobs. Asked what he considered to be the biggest problem with the Montgomery police, a high-ranking official of the Alabama State Troopers replied, without hesitation, "They have too many young officers because they don't pay enough to keep experienced men."

SEVERAL HIGHLY SYMBOLIC CHANGES have been made in the police force since Folmar became mayor. One was the repainting of all the police cars from a pleasant, non-threatening light blue to stark black and white. Another was the emergence of black SWAT-team style uniforms for officers on the night shifts. The new uniforms replace the traditional policeman's hat with a baseball-type cap without a badge and feature bloused pants tucked into high lace-up military-style boots. The people inside the cars and uniforms are the same as before, but the difference in appearance is striking and ominous.

Ex-police say the night shift officers themselves sought the new uniform because they believed it would be safer during the most dangerous hours of police work—a shiny badge flashing in the night is a better target. But the uniform adds to the military effect which Folmar has encouraged for the department, and the change has not gone unnoticed in the community. The uniforms were meant to be worn by the third-shift officers, but the hats, at least, have apparently been adopted as a symbol by some officers, especially the younger ones, and are routinely seen at all hours. Some older officers even doubt the theory behind the new uniforms. "When we're out on the street," they say, "we want people to recognize instantly that we're police"; and the traditional uniform tells them that.

It is impossible to judge the accuracy of the allegation, but people who say they have been harassed by Montgomery police, especially young blacks, say in so many words that they believe there are certain police or even squads of police who look for opportunities to provoke people, and that these are the police who wear the military-type uniforms. This may only be a perception, but it increases fear and hostility and that creates trouble for the officer on patrol. The state trooper official who spoke of low salaries mentioned a second area of concern for Montgomery police: "P.R.—they've also got a public relations problem. Brother, do they need some better public relations."

Even the ex-officers who are critical of the mayor, however, also note that he reorganized the department into smaller divisions with greater supervision and more officers on the street at all times. Folmar and Chief Swindall claim that crime has been reduced since Folmar took charge.

A city government source from the Robinson era observed that Folmar took office at a time when, due to the Whitehurst scandal, police relations with blacks were at a low point. And then, rather than take steps to identify and correct the problem, it seems that Folmar's actions made things worse.

Not all of Folmar's strong-arm tactics were aimed specifically at the black community. Soon after he took office the police conducted an illegal drug search of patrons at a rock concert at the Montgomery Civic Center. Every person entering was searched, with or without probable cause, and a number of arrests were made. The arrests were nullified after a federal judge sharply rebuked the police actions—and the mayor—but three years would pass before another rock concert was held at the Civic Center.

City hall insiders also view with suspicion the scuttling by Folmar of the reorganization that former mayor Robinson had engineered. Basically, Robinson divided the city's departments into several major divisions, each of which was headed by a professional administrator who took care of the details and answered to the mayor's office on policy and procedure. Folmar has dismantled this system and every department head in the city is under Folmar's personal supervision—and knows it.

SUCH IS THE BACKGROUND against which the current racial troubles in Montgomery must be seen. Legal challenges have been raised to a Folmar-backed redistricting plan for this year's city elections. A federal judge has agreed with black challengers that the city's new reapportionment plan was drawn to discriminate against black voters and black office holders, particularly against long-time Folmar opponent Joe

Reed. After the ruling, Folmar said the city would appeal, and he also issued what amounted to a personal attack on the federal judge, who is black. Folmar's statement, to the effect that the ruling was not unexpected considering the source, encouraged disrespect for the law and for federal judges and bordered on outright racism. Elections may or may not be held in October.

Despite widespread discontent with Folmar, few have seemed especially eager to challenge him. The strongest potential candidate has been city council president Peak, but he has said he will not run. The announced candidates to date are a young white businesswoman who said she would drop out if a more experienced contender emerged, a white contractor with connections to the business community, and Franklin James, a member of a prominent Montgomery family and the brother of former longtime mayor Earl James. Only James, who was once the state's industrial relations director, has any political experience. James announced his candidacy just as this issue was going to press, and it is too early to assess his chances. However, his political reflexes are evidently in good shape because he went directly to the key issue: Folmar himself. James's opening statement included references to the incumbent's ego, grandstanding tactics, and lightning-rod administrative style. Montgomery needs a mayor, James said, who can get along with all of the city's people, and who solves problems rather than creates them. James also promised that his industrial relations background would bring factories and jobs.

Black council member Donald Watkins, an attorney who represented the Bernard Whitehurst family after the 1976 shooting, has said he will run against Folmar if "no credible white candidate comes forward." (The statement was made before James or the contractor, David Thames, announced their intentions; Watkins has not indicated whether he considers Thames or James to be credible candidates.)

Blacks acknowledge that no black mayoral candidate can win in the face of a white electoral majority. However, the precinct totals cannot be comforting to Folmar. He cannot be expected to get more than a handful of Montgomery's black voters, and 30.2 percent of the registered voters are black. He is also a Republican, and although the city elections in Montgomery are not partisan contests, he would still be vulnerable against a strong white Democrat who can avoid antagonizing the conservatives while still expressing some of the misgivings many whites also feel toward Folmar's brand of leadership. Folmar did not carry Montgomery in the 1982 gubernatorial race against George Wallace.

FOLMAR RECENTLY PRESENTED PETITIONS bearing what he said were more than seventeen thousand signatures of Montgomery voters who wanted him to run for reelection. However, no one has collected the signatures of those who will vote for *anyone* else, and Folmar is obviously sniffing the political winds. While he had earlier rejected calls for committees to probe issues caus-

ing racial tensions, he changed his course a few weeks ago and announced his own bi-racial committee. He appointed the chairman and vice-chairman and invited council members to nominate three persons each to the new committee. So far, three of the four black council members have declined, saying the committee was created   *Commissioner John Knight.*

Johnnie R. Carr.

by Folmar for political reasons and could never be effective while the chairman was appointed by Folmar. Critics also say that Folmar made a mistake when he named a white chairman and a black vice-chairman rather than two co-chairs, and they view the structure of the committee as proof of Folmar's determination to control even the discussion over Montgomery's current problems. The committee received another wound when the black vice-chairman, the president of predominantly black Alabama State University, resigned without attending a meeting, saying he could not take part in a committee with such obviously political overtones.

Meanwhile, an anonymous citizen known as Jack Smith has created the Friendly Supper Club, which merely invites interested persons to show up with a guest of a different race at an appointed time at a local cafeteria to "break bread together" and to get to know one another across racial lines.

The second of the dinners, in June, took place just one day after a cross was burned in the yard of black county commissioner John Knight, who is the spokesman for the boycott called by blacks against First Alabama Bank. Coming at a time of increasing attention to Montgomery's racial troubles, the contrast between the cross-burning and the Friendly Supper Club was too great for the media to pass up. CBS and NBC both sent camera crews to town, and their reports juxtaposed pictures of the charred cross in Knight's yard with shots of blacks and whites smiling and talking around cafeteria tables. The local media especially made a point of the difference between Folmar's beleaguered biracial committee and the independently created Friendly Supper Club. Dialogue was the order of the day, but it was not the Mayor who was doing the talking.

One of those at the June dinner was Johnnie Carr, the president of the Montgomery Improvement Association, which sponsored the bus boycott in 1955–56. Dialogue is fine, said Mrs. Carr, but it is not the solution. "When a city of this size can't find a decent leader for mayor, I have to ask what is wrong. Folmar accuses us of crying 'racism,' but when you look at the man's record, how do you explain it except as racism?"

Mrs. Carr said the black community views Folmar's creation of the bi-racial committee as a belated attempt to gloss over the current problems. She believes the strategy will not work.

"We don't need a band-aid," she said. "We need a good physical examination, and then we're going to have to do some political surgery."

~

Aftermath, 2025

Within a month after the February 27, 1983, "Todd Road Incident," the charges against most of the black mourners were dismissed. In one case, there was a mistrial. There were no convictions.

Montgomery Advertiser reporter Alvin Benn had by then already traveled to Michigan and interviewed defendants' family members and others and checked police records. His reporting showed that those accused of being "animals" were well-respected, hard-working churchgoers and family people in their home communities.

Emory Folmar continued to serve as mayor of Montgomery until he was defeated in 1999. He died in 2011 without holding elective office again, though he did serve as the appointed head of the Alabama Alcoholic Beverage Control board.

Charles Swindall served as Montgomery police chief until he was succeeded by Folmar protege John Wilson. Swindall died in 1992.

The mayor's appointed biracial committee quickly foundered and was replaced by One Montgomery, an independent interracial discussion group with a broad membership that continues to meet weekly.

Another Todd Road response was the sponsorship by three white businessmen and a black lawyer of Leadership Montgomery, a city-wide education program that graduated its first class in 1984. In its annual nine-month sessions, thousands of Montgomerians have learned about city history, structure, operations, arts, culture, and each other.

The Friendly Supper Club met the first Monday of every month from May 1983 until Covid shut down group dinners in 2020.

About the Author

Horace Randall Williams was founder and editor of the independent book publisher Black Belt Press, and then he was editor-in-chief of NewSouth Books, which he co-founded with publisher Suzanne La Rosa in 2000 (the imprint was sold in 2022 to the University of Georgia Press). Since his first book in 1989, he has edited, published, and/or co-published more than 900 titles, which is believed to be more than any other general trade book editor and publisher in Alabama history. Under his own name, he's also the author, co-author, or editor of a dozen books. Before book publishing, he was a reporter, editor, and publisher for newspapers and magazines, and he worked a decade at the Southern Poverty Law Center, where he was the founding director of the Klanwatch Project. He is also the founder of the Capri Community Film Society, a graduate of Leadership Montgomery, and for more than two decades was a board member of the Montgomery Improvement Association, the organization created to coordinate the Montgomery Bus Boycott of 1955–56. He's a native of LaFayette, Alabama, a graduate of LaFayette High School and Samford University, and he lives in Montgomery.